GREG LOUGANIS
Diving for Gold

GREG LOUGANIS
Diving for Gold

By Joyce Milton

With photographs

Illustrations by Stephen Marchesi

STEP-UP BOOKS

Random House 🏠 New York

Photo credits: pp. 1, 2, 65, 67, Focus on Sports; p. 17, Skip Fenn/La Mesa Recreation; pp. 28, 31, 33, 40, 44, 45, 63, 74, 76, 79, 81, 82, 83, 84, 87, AP/Wide World Photos; p. 39, UPI/Bettmann Newsphotos; p. 50, Richard Mackson/*Sports Illustrated*; pp. 53, 55, Bill Eppridge/*Sports Illustrated*; p. 61, David Madison/Duomo; p. 69, Neil Leifer/*Time* magazine.

Cover photo: Copyright © 1988 by Pascal Rondeau/Allsport

Library of Congress Cataloging-in-Publication Data:
Milton, Joyce. Greg Louganis: diving for gold. (Step-up books) SUMMARY: A biography of the champion diver who has won more titles, including several Olympic medals, than anyone in diving history to date. ISBN: 0-394-84586-2 (pbk.); 0-394-94586-7 (lib. bdg.) 1. Louganis, Greg, 1960– .
— Juvenile literature. 2. Divers—United States—Biography—Juvenile literature. 3. Olympics—Juvenile literature. [1. Louganis, Greg, 1960– . 2. Divers. 3. Olympics] I. Title. GV838.L68M55 1989 797.2'4'0924 [B] [92] 88-35670

Manufactured in the United States of America 1 2 3 4 5 6 7 8 9 10

90-120

GREG LOUGANIS

Diving for Gold

1.

Greg Louganis sailed off the diving board and did a flip in midair. He landed with a big splash. It was not a very good dive. But nine-year-old Greg was just learning. With a few quick strokes he swam to the side of the pool. He could hardly wait to try the same stunt again.

After he climbed out of the pool, Greg returned to the board. This time he jumped down on the board extra hard as he took off. Up, up, up he went. It was like flying.

The only problem was that this time his mother saw the dive. The backyard pool had just been put in a little while ago. Greg had promised his parents that he wouldn't do any tricky stuff. What would happen now? Would his mother forbid him to use the pool? No. Greg's parents decided on diving lessons instead. If Greg was going to dive, they wanted him to do it the right way.

A few days later Greg showed up at the town recreation center to take his first diving lesson. He was a shy boy who did not have any friends at school. He was not a good student. Kids called him retard, and when grownups talked to him, he often did not answer.

As Greg lined up with the rest of the beginners' class, the diving teacher did not pay him any special attention. The teacher had no way of knowing that his new student would one day be the best diver in history.

2.

Greg Louganis was born in California in 1960. His father had come to California from Samoa, an island in the Pacific Ocean. He had black hair and light-brown skin. Greg's mother had grown up in California. She had blond hair and blue eyes. Both of Greg's parents were very young. They had no money, and they were not married.

When Greg was a few months old, his mother made a hard decision. She had no job. She couldn't see how she could give her baby the care he needed. She decided that he would be better off if she gave him up for adoption.

Greg was lucky to be adopted by a loving family. His new parents were Peter and Frances

Louganis. Peter Louganis worked for a company that owned fishing boats.

The Louganises already had one adopted child. Her name was Despina, and she was part American Indian.

Despina took dancing lessons. She was bright and athletic. From the time Greg learned to walk, he wanted to do everything Despina did.

One day Mrs. Louganis came into the living room. She found Greg standing on his head in the middle of the room. He wasn't even two years old yet! The next time Despina had dancing class, Greg's mother decided to take him along to watch.

Soon Greg was the star of the class. He was so good that a year later he got a lead role in the class recital.

On the day of the recital three-year-old Greg dressed up in a little tuxedo and top hat. His partner was a four-year-old girl. Greg sang a song called "Dance with Me." Then he and the little girl did a tap dance.

Beyond the stage lights were row after row of unfamiliar faces. Greg began to belt out the words to the song. He was really enjoying himself now.

When the music ended, the audience burst into applause. Greg didn't want the golden moment to end, so he sat down right on the edge of the stage and listened to all the clapping. Finally Greg's teacher had to come out and take him away. It was the only way to get Greg off the stage!

3.

By the time he started school, Greg had appeared in several more dancing recitals. Greg was always the star of the show. He loved being the center of attention. He seemed to light up in front of an audience.

The people who saw Greg perform would never have guessed that he was a little boy with a lot of problems. But it was true.

Greg's problems had started as soon as he was old enough to go out to play by himself. Like his Samoan father, Greg had brown skin and dark-brown eyes. All the other kids in the neighborhood seemed to be blond and blue eyed. They teased Greg about his looks.

Some of the kids were really nasty. "Nigger!" they shouted. "Get out of here! We don't want to play with you!"

Greg was surprised and hurt. He didn't know what to say or do. The Louganises were the only family he could remember. If he did not belong with them, in his own neighborhood, where did he belong?

He began to stutter. Sometimes when he started to speak, his tongue seemed to get stuck on one letter.

"Don't you talk to me like that!" he would try to say.

But all that came out was "D . . . . don't you t . . . t . . . t . . . ."

His stuttering gave kids a new excuse to tease Greg. They called him a sissy and a big baby.

If Despina was around, she would finish Greg's sentences for him. She only wanted to help. But Greg got tired of having his sister talk for him.

Because of his stutter Greg didn't go out to play very often. It was easier to stay home. Even so, Greg was looking forward to starting school.

After all, he was the star pupil of his dancing class. Maybe he would be a star in school, too.

But first grade was a terrible disappointment.

The worst part of the day was reading time. As the teacher passed out the books, Greg would sink down in his seat.

And when the teacher called on him to read out loud, he wished he could just disappear.

Greg did the best he could: "I . . . was . . . a . . . c . . . c . . . c . . . cat," he would read.

By this time the other kids were all laughing.

"I *saw* a cat," the teacher corrected him. "Not I *was* a cat."

Greg nodded, but reading was so hard for him. When he looked at a word, the letters seemed all mixed up. Sometimes he read words backward. Sometimes the letters did not make any sense at all.

Now the kids had a new nickname for Greg— "Dummy." They thought he was stupid. And Greg figured they must be right.

4.

It wasn't like Greg to sit around moping. He made up for his troubles in school by spending more time dancing. He took gymnastics classes too. When he was six years old, Greg could already do a back flip!

And when Greg was nine, he started to take diving lessons. At the pool he felt good about himself. He never had troubles there the way he did at school. He could do everything the coach wanted—and more.

By the time he was in fifth grade, Greg was already competing in diving meets.

The recreation center that he attended had a good diving team. Greg was one of the young-

During the years when he took lessons at La Mesa, Greg (second row, far right) traveled to many meets with his coach and other divers.

est divers on it. But he soon became one of the best.

Why was he so good?

For one thing Greg was stronger than most boys his age. He had powerful muscles in his legs. When he went off the edge of the diving board, he got a good, high jump. This meant he was in the air a split second longer than the other divers. He had more time to do his dive before he hit the water.

Being strong is only part of being a good diver. In competition a diver is supposed to look smooth, never jerky.

"Diving is like poetry," Greg's coach used to tell the team.

This was hard for a lot of the kids on the team to understand. But Greg had learned to be graceful from his dancing lessons. When he practiced a dive, he thought about a song he liked. The music he heard in his head helped him to get the timing right.

One test of a good dive is how the diver looks when he goes into the water. If the diver's body is straight, he will not make a big splash. This is called "ripping it."

Greg would work on the same dive over and over. Soon he made hardly any splash at all. "Rip it, Greggo!" his teammates would shout.

When Greg heard that, he would smile. Greg was a quiet boy. When he did a great dive, he didn't make a big deal out of it. But he didn't have to. His diving did his talking for him.

Greg enjoyed practicing. But he was not so sure that he liked taking part in diving meets. The competition was stiff. There was a lot of pressure to win. The pressure was especially hard on a shy boy like Greg. He hated to have so many people watching him when he made a mistake.

Greg's mother made him feel better. She used to come to see him compete. When Greg didn't get his dives right, he didn't say much. But his mother knew how bad he felt. "Just remember," she told him. "I'll still love you, win or lose."

Greg decided to keep on competing. When he was only eleven years old, he was picked to go to the Junior Olympics in Colorado. The Junior Olympics were a kind of training ground for the U.S. Olympic team. Every year the best young athletes in all different sports from all over the country were picked to take part in the Junior Olympics. Greg was proud to be included.

But he was nervous, too. Most of the athletes were in high school. Greg was one of the youngest kids there. Still, Greg did well in his events. He was better than the other boys his age. He was even better than the boys who were thirteen and fourteen years old!

After the Junior Olympics, Greg was known as one of the best young divers in America. It was a very exciting time for him. He was invited to take part in meets all over the country. When he was thirteen, he even got to go to Europe to compete against some of the best junior divers in the world. Greg still got nervous sometimes when he was in a meet. But so were the other divers. Greg was the one who was making them nervous!

5.

By the time he was a teenager, Greg was leading a double life. At the pool he was a star. He was on his way to being a world-class diver.

But at school he was still considered a dummy. Many of Greg's classmates did not even know about his diving! To them he was just a strange, quiet boy who hardly ever talked in class. By now he was years behind the other kids in reading. Greg didn't know why he had such trouble in school. All he knew was that he hated being called names.

Greg's father wanted him to fight back against the kids who tormented him. He made Greg go to wrestling class so he could learn to defend himself. But Greg hated wrestling. Maybe it was because the classes were his father's idea. He needed to find his own answers to his problems.

Greg quit wrestling. He saved his money and bought himself a pet boa constrictor. When he walked around town, he carried the big snake around his neck. Some of the other kids Greg's age were afraid of Greg's pet snake. At first he was afraid of it too. But one of his reasons for buying the snake was to overcome his fear.

Greg made himself take good care of his pet. He fed it rats that he bought at the pet store. Soon Greg grew to like his snake. Showing it made him feel good about himself.

After school and on weekends, Greg was very busy. Besides diving practice and going to meets, he was working part time.

Diving lessons cost money. So did traveling to meets in other parts of the country. Some of Greg's teammates came from wealthy families. But the Louganises were not rich. Greg's parents expected him to work to help pay his way.

As soon as he was old enough, Greg got a part-time job. He worked on the docks for the fishing company where his father worked. Greg's job was mending fishing nets.

The nets were heavy. Lifting and carrying them around was like working out with weights. When he came home at night, Greg was exhausted. But all that lifting helped Greg grow stronger than ever. The muscles in his back and shoulders became very powerful.

Greg was changing in other ways too. He was determined to make friends at school. But the only kids who accepted him were the ones in the wild crowd. His new friends all drank and smoked. So Greg started smoking and drinking

to fit in. He looked for places where he could sneak a drink of wine. He even had a bottle hidden in his school locker!

His parents were worried about him. Mr. Louganis was afraid that Greg was headed for serious trouble.

Greg's diving was a special gift. Greg had worked hard at it. But maybe Greg's talent was so special, he needed an even bigger challenge.

One day Mr. Louganis went to see a well-known diving coach. The coach's name was Dr. Sammy Lee.

Dr. Lee ran a diving club that trained at the recreation center in Mission Viejo, California. Some of the top swimmers and divers in the world trained at Mission Viejo.

Years before, Dr. Lee had seen Greg dive at the Junior Olympics. He had told Greg and his family then that Greg had what it took to win an Olympic gold medal. All he needed was the right training. "Greg is the best diver I've ever seen," Dr. Lee had said then.

Mr. Louganis remembered Dr. Lee's words. He thought training for the Olympics would give his son a goal to work toward. It would keep him away from his wild friends.

Mr. Louganis just wasn't sure the family could afford to hire a coach like Dr. Lee. "How much money do you want to coach my son?" he asked him.

Dr. Lee's answer came as a surprise. "None," he said. "I'll do it for love."

6.

Greg was lucky to work with Dr. Lee. From the beginning Dr. Lee encouraged Greg to set high goals for himself.

The Olympic Games were held just once every four years. The 1976 Games in Montreal, Canada, were a little more than a year away. But Dr. Lee told Greg that if he worked very hard, he would be able to make the U.S. team. He might even be good enough to win a gold medal!

So what if Greg didn't have a lot of friends? So what if he felt lonely a lot of the time? Dr. Lee knew all about loneliness. He hadn't let being lonely stop him from reaching his goals. And he didn't think it would stop Greg, either.

Dr. Sammy Lee was a Korean-American.

When he was a boy, during the 1940s, the United States was involved in World War II. Japan was an enemy. Some people had the idea that Japanese-Americans were spies. Sammy Lee was not even a Japanese-American. But many people could not tell the difference between a Korean and a Japanese.

Sammy Lee had a dream of becoming a diver. He used to attend swimming and diving meets whenever he had the chance. More than once people called him a spy. No one could say why spies would be interested in diving meets. But that is what some people thought. They even reported Sammy Lee to the FBI.

More than once strangers tried to goad Sammy Lee into fighting. They could afford to be brave. Sammy was only five feet tall!

Being so unpopular just made Sammy Lee more determined. He had two goals. One was to be a doctor. The other was to win a gold medal in the Olympics.

Many people told Sammy he could not do both. He disagreed. "If you think that," he told one teacher, "you do not know Sammy Lee."

In 1948 Sammy Lee won a gold medal in diving in the Olympics. He won another gold medal in 1952. Then he went to medical school. He did well and became a successful doctor. But

Sammy Lee's Olympic dream came true in 1948 when he won the gold medal in platform diving. (Sammy Lee is in the center.)

Dr. Lee never lost his interest in diving. He still spent a lot of time training young divers with special talent.

When Greg started training with Dr. Lee, he had to agree to follow some strict rules. There would be no smoking. And no drinking. When he wasn't training at the sports center, Greg put in long hours in Dr. Lee's backyard pool. Sometimes he practiced until ten o'clock at night.

So that he would have as much time as possible for training, Greg moved in with Dr. Lee and his wife. He learned to like the Korean food that Mrs. Lee served. In his free time he helped Mrs. Lee cook and kept the swimming pool clean. Dr. Lee expected his students to help out to pay him back for the time he spent training them. Greg didn't mind the work. Dr. and Mrs. Lee had become like a second family to him.

7.

To get ready for the Olympics, Greg had to practice two different kinds of diving.

The first is called springboard diving. The competitors dive off a diving board. In the Olympics divers go off a three-meter springboard—that's about ten feet above the water.

The second part of Olympic diving competition is called platform diving. The platform is usually a concrete tower. The Olympic platform is ten meters high. Ten meters is about thirty-three feet.

Diving off the ten-meter platform can be scary. And not just for beginners! By the time a platform diver hits the water, his body is flying through the air at over thirty miles an hour. A diver who makes a bad mistake can wind up seriously injured.

Greg had dived off platforms before. He wasn't afraid of heights. But Olympic platform diving was a big challenge. To have a chance to win, he would have to learn new dives, harder and more dangerous than any he had done before.

The 10-meter platform is always a challenge. But Greg soon developed championship form.

Standing on the ten-meter platform, Greg thought the pool looked tiny! He could see straight to the bottom. That was almost fifty feet down!

Dr. Lee had a list of new moves for Greg to practice. There were forward somersaults. And backward somersaults. And midair twists. To do some of the new dives, Greg had to start by doing a handstand on the edge of the platform.

When divers are spinning through the air, it is easy for them to get confused. They are not sure how far away the water is. Sometimes they can't tell which way is down. Greg knew that he would have to train himself to "spot" the water on every dive. Luckily he was a little bit bowlegged. When he was doing a somersault, he could peek through the space between his knees and see the water. Being bowlegged turned out to be an advantage as a diver!

Most of the divers Dr. Lee had trained had big egos. They liked to brag about how good they were. But Greg was different. He didn't talk about himself much. And he didn't seem

Some of the trickiest dives start with a handstand on the edge of the platform.

to take himself very seriously. If he didn't do a dive quite right, he would laugh at himself.

Dr. Lee sometimes wondered if Greg really cared enough about winning. "You've got to have the killer instinct to be a winner," he would say.

Was that true? If so, did Greg have what it took to be a world champion? Soon Greg would find out.

It was time for the Olympic trials. The best divers in the United States were all there. Only the top finishers would get to go on to Montreal.

The other divers at the trials were surprised that a sixteen-year-old like Greg was there at all. They still thought of him as a little kid—a junior diver.

The older divers had worked for years to get their chance to go to the Olympics. Some of them resented Greg. They felt he didn't deserve a spot on the team. He didn't have enough experience to win against the world's best divers. The other divers complained about Greg behind his back. He would have his chance four years from now, in 1980. Why was he in such a hurry?

Greg knew what the other divers were saying about him. But he pretended not to notice. He just went ahead and did his best. When the trials were over, he had won both the springboard *and* the platform events.

He was on his way to Montreal.

8.

Going to the Olympics was Greg's dream come true. The best athletes in the world were all there. The fastest runners. The strongest weightlifters. The top amateur basketball and volleyball players. All the athletes lived together in special dormitories built just for the Olympic Games. They ate together in a big cafeteria. Newspaper and TV reporters followed the best-known stars around, asking them questions. Many of the events were shown on TV all around the world.

Everywhere Greg went, he sensed the excitement swirling all around him. But he did not really feel a part of it all.

Some of the other American divers still were not sure he deserved to be on the team. They thought his win in the trial was just luck. They didn't think he could stand up to Olympic pressure. Maybe the only way he could prove himself was to win a gold medal.

Worse yet, Dr. Lee was not an official Olympic coach. At first he wasn't even allowed to come to the side of the pool to give Greg advice.

Greg was on his own. In the Olympic Village, where all the athletes stayed, he had no one to talk to. He kept to himself. He hardly ever smiled.

The springboard contest was the first Olympic diving event. Greg did not do very well. He made the finals, but just barely. On the last day of the event he took sixth place. This was pretty good for a sixteen-year-old. But it was a big disappointment for the U.S. team. And for Greg, too.

Diving had always been one of the United States's strongest Olympic sports. The American divers were expected to do well. Now some of the other divers thought they had been right about Greg. They said the older divers he had beaten at the trials would have finished higher than sixth place. Maybe they were right.

Next came the platform diving. Now the pressure was really on Greg. He was competing against the best diver in the world. He was an Italian named Klaus Dibiasi, but everyone called him by his nickname, "The Blond Angel." Like Dr. Lee, Klaus Dibiasi had won the gold medal twice—in 1968 and 1972. He was the favorite to win again in 1976.

"You've got to stop Klaus," Dr. Lee told Greg. "Do it for America."

Greg wanted to win and was going to try his hardest. But he was still a kid. Did he really have a chance to to beat the Blond Angel? First Greg had to get through the preliminary competition. This time he had no trouble placing among the top ten finalists.

In the finalists' round, the scores from the preliminaries didn't count. All ten finalists started out even. Each of them had to do ten dives. And for each dive, the judges would award from one to ten points. The highest score and the lowest score were thrown out. The rest of the judges' scores would be added together.

Of course, some dives were a lot harder than others. So each dive also had a rating. A dive with a three rating was a lot harder than a dive with a two rating.

The scoring system was complicated. Greg couldn't play it safe. It wasn't enough to do easy dives well. To have a chance of winning, he had to do the riskiest dives. And do them well.

Greg chose to do some very tricky and challenging dives. It would be very easy to make a mistake. But after eight dives, Greg was in second place. He had a chance to beat the Blond Angel.

Greg's ninth dive was especially tough. He had to do three and a half somersaults in midair. Then he had to finish the somersaults in time to straighten out his body before he hit the water.

Greg stepped to the end of the platform. When

he was ready, he leaped into his dive. He got through the somersaults. But his timing was off a little. He didn't get his legs straightened out, and he hit the water with a big splash.

The judges put up their scores. Greg got mostly fives. In diving, a ten is a perfect score. A seven is good. A five is not very good at all. Especially not in the Olympics.

In just a few seconds, he had ruined his chances for a gold medal.

At the age of 16, Greg was competing for an Olympic medal.

But he came back for his tenth dive, and he did it well. In fact, it was one of the best dives of his life. When the event was over, Greg Louganis had finished second.

He had won an Olympic medal! Not the gold — that went to Klaus Dibiasi — but the silver.

When Greg (on the left) lost the gold medal to Klaus Dibiasi (on the right), he tried not to show his disappointment.

Suddenly Greg was surrounded by cameras. TV reporters fired questions at him. They thought it was wonderful that a boy still in high school had won an Olympic medal.

Even Klaus Dibiasi thought Greg was special. The Blond Angel was planning to retire before the next Olympics. He told Greg that he expected him to win the gold medal at the next Olympics, coming up in Moscow in 1980. "In Moscow, I'll be watching you," he said.

Greg smiled and thanked Dibiasi. But inside he felt terrible. If only he hadn't missed that one dive!

No matter what Dr. Lee said, Greg was convinced that he had let his coach down. He had let the U.S. team down too. If one of the more experienced American divers had come to Montreal instead of him, the U.S. might have won a gold medal.

Greg kept his disappointment to himself. But it was a letdown he would never forget. "I felt my life was over," he said later.

9.

For a while it seemed as if the silver would be Greg's first and only medal. After Montreal, Greg didn't enjoy diving. Luck seemed to have turned against him. He sprained his back while he was training. His muscles hurt when he hit the water.

Everyone expected the new Olympic medal winner to be the top diver in the United States. But in 1977 Greg did not do well at the meet that was held to pick the American champion. He came in second in the platform. In springboard he was fifteenth!

After that Greg stopped coming to practice. He told Dr. Lee he needed time off.

Being an Olympic medal winner hadn't solved Greg's other problems either. In fact, training for the Olympics had left him further behind in his schoolwork than ever. And he still didn't have many friends.

Maybe the other kids thought Greg was stuck up. After all, he was a celebrity. He had an Olympic medal at home!

Greg needed someone to talk to. Soon he was hanging around with the wild crowd again. He was drinking beer and wine. He was smoking cigarettes.

Then in 1978 a new coach joined the staff at Mission Viejo. Dr. Lee no longer had time to work with divers every day. He was semiretired from coaching. The new coach was Ron O'Brien. And he was not about to give up on Greg Louganis.

Ron O'Brien wasn't sure what he had to teach Greg. But he did see that Greg needed to learn to enjoy diving again. He convinced Greg to come back to practice.

Greg and his new coach, Ron O'Brien, became a longstanding team.

"Diving is supposed to be *fun,*" Ron O'Brien kept reminding Greg.

Ron O'Brien was part friend, part coach. He brought back the thrill of diving for Greg. And soon Greg was training as hard as ever.

All the hard work paid off. Nineteen seventy-eight was a good year for Greg. For the first time he won a world championship in diving. He came in first in the platform event. The man he beat was the Blond Angel.

Eighteen-year-old Greg, on his way to winning his first world championship.

Greg also graduated from high school that year. He still had trouble reading. But he had begun to get better. Greg didn't know why, but he often saw letters in reverse. The letters *s-a-w* still sometimes looked like *w-a-s*. Working on his own, he taught himself to read the same word

45

forward and backward until he could guess what it was supposed to be. By doing this, he was able to raise his reading scores.

Greg even got into college. He started his first year at the University of Miami.

One day during his freshman year Greg found a new word on a vocabulary list: Dyslexia. He looked it up. He found that it was the name of a special reading problem. People with this problem had trouble seeing words. One way to tell dyslexics was that they often read words backward.

Greg was amazed. That sounded just like him!

For the first time Greg had a name for his problem. He learned that there were ways to overcome dyslexia. Greg had already figured out some of those ways on his own. Now he was able to make even more progress. Soon he was actually enjoying reading. He began taking courses in literature. They were among his favorite classes.

Greg had shown that he was one of the best divers in the world. He could hardly wait for the next Olympic Games. They were going to be held in Moscow in 1980. Everyone said Greg would be a sure thing to win a gold medal. Maybe even two.

But when it came to winning Olympic gold, it still seemed that luck was working against him.

In 1979 Greg went to the Soviet Union for a special meet. This was his chance to size up the Soviet divers he would be competing against in the Moscow Olympics. But this meet was not held in Moscow. It took place in a smaller city, one that did not have the best equipment for diving.

The American divers noticed right away that the platform used for the meet felt different. Platforms are usually made of concrete. This one was wood. It bounced when a diver jumped on it.

The wooden platform made it hard for the divers to take off correctly. Greg had no trouble until his third dive. That was when he made a serious mistake. He didn't jump out far enough.

On the way down, his head hit the edge of the platform. *Thud!*

Greg was knocked out. He fell like a stone all the way to the pool below.

People jumped into the pool and dragged Greg from the water. His eyes were closed. He didn't wake up for fifteen minutes. An ambulance rushed him to the hospital.

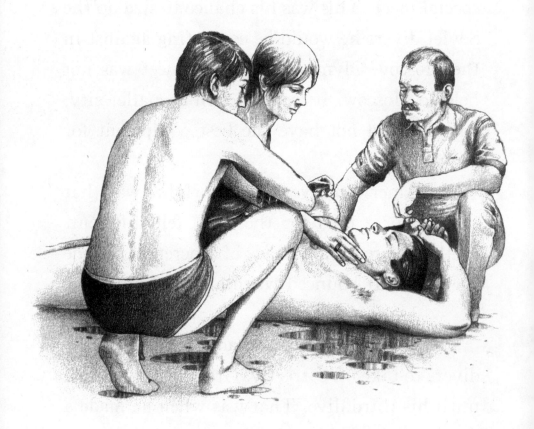

Greg's accident was serious. But he was determined not to let it stop his training for the Moscow Games. He left the hospital the next morning. Just two days later he started diving again.

It seemed that everything that could go wrong had already happened. But not quite. One night, after Greg returned home to the United States, he heard some terrible news. The Soviet Union had invaded Afghanistan, a country just to its south. The United States government was very unhappy about this. To protest the invasion, President Carter decided that American athletes would not take part in the Moscow Olympics.

Like all the American athletes, Greg was heartbroken. Many had given up jobs and school to train for the Moscow Games. There would not be another Olympics for four years. That was a long time away. Now Greg had a tough decision to make. Could he afford to keep on training for so many years? He had been planning to retire after the Moscow Games. He had given a lot of thought to what he would do after diving. His dream was to become a professional dancer or an actor. To succeed in either career, he had to start while he was still young. But Greg wasn't ready to give up on his Olympic dreams. Not yet. He decided to keep diving a little longer.

Greg never forgot his love of dancing.

Greg's decision meant sacrifices. To be near Coach O'Brien, he had to drop out of college in Miami and move back to California. To earn money, he took a job in a Mexican restaurant.

After a few months Greg was offered a scholarship by the University of California. He started taking classes again.

Had he made the right decision? Could he keep on training until 1984? Greg wasn't sure. The sport of diving was getting more competitive all the time. Younger divers were coming along every year. There was a lot of pressure to keep doing harder, more dangerous dives. Sure, Greg was the best right now. But how long could he stay on top?

10.

One day in 1982 Greg stood at the end of the ten-meter platform. Thirty-three feet down, at poolside, Coach O'Brien was shouting.

"You can stay up there all day if you want!" he yelled. "You can have lunch there. And breakfast, too, for all I care. But you won't come down until you do that dive!"

It wasn't like Ron O'Brien to shout. And it wasn't like Greg Louganis to be scared. But this dive was different. It was so new that no one had ever done it in a diving meet. Greg was hoping to be the first.

The new dive was called an inward—or reverse—three and a half tuck. Greg had done three and a half somersaults before. But this time he had to turn *toward* the platform. That was much scarier.

As always, when Greg started to learn a new dive, he practiced it on dry land first. To do this he wore a special belt around his waist. The belt was attached to ropes that hung from pulleys attached to a rigging of tall poles. The ropes were controlled by Coach O'Brien. The ground underneath the rigging was covered with soft mats.

Greg practiced the midair somersaults while hanging from the rigging. He tried them over and over again. But doing the same moves off the platform was different. There was nothing to save him if he made a mistake.

Coach O'Brien refused to let Greg give up. Finally Greg knew he had to make his move. He held his head straight and his arms out. Then he made his leap.

Greg turned over. One . . . two . . . three . . . and a half times. Then he spotted the water, and in he went.

Divers talk about using their hands to "punch a hole" in the water. If they do it right, they make hardly any splash.

Greg had done it right. He had "punched a hole" in the water. He came out of the pool smiling. As time went on, the reverse three and a half became one of his best dives.

By 1982 Greg was diving better than ever. He won the world championship, not just in platform but in the three-meter springboard,

When Greg went into the water, he hardly made any splash at all.

too. The list of titles he had won was getting longer all the time.

But he was still drinking wine and beer. And he was still smoking cigarettes. Greg liked to think that other divers didn't know about his bad habits. After he finished a practice session, he would go out to his car and sneak a smoke.

One day, on his way out of the recreation center, Greg ran into one of the junior divers in the parking lot. The boy wasn't even in his teens yet, but he was puffing away on a cigarette.

"What's going on?" Greg asked.

The boy was not at all embarrassed to be caught smoking. "I know you smoke," he told Greg. "And I want to be just like you."

Greg didn't say anything. But the boy's words hurt. It had never occurred to him that younger divers looked up to him. That was a big responsibility.

Greg talked to his friends about why he needed to smoke and drink. He also talked to Ron O'Brien and his wife. These habits didn't make sense for someone who wanted to be a winning athlete. Greg realized that deep inside he wasn't sure he deserved to be a winner.

But the time had come to change that. So Greg gave up cigarettes and beer. He started to learn to relax and make friends. He started going around to schools to give talks. He asked kids not to drink and smoke. Another thing he said was "It's okay to be shy." Stop worrying about being the most popular boy or girl in the class, he told the kids. Just enjoy being yourself.

11.

Greg wasn't the only one working on new, more difficult dives. In 1983 he went to an important meet in Canada. One of the other divers was a Russian. Like Greg, he had been working on a platform dive that called for three and a half reverse somersaults.

During the week before the finals, the divers practiced at the same pool. All week long the Russian diver had trouble with his new dive. Finally it was time for him to do it for the judges.

The Russian was supposed to dive right before Greg. Greg climbed to a platform halfway up the tower and waited for his turn. The Russian started his dive. Suddenly Greg had a bad feeling. He turned his back to the pool. He closed his eyes and covered his ears. Then he felt the tower shake.

The Russian diver had hit the platform on his way down. When Greg opened his eyes, there was blood in the pool.

The Russian diver was rushed to the hospital. Minutes later Greg had to go out on the board and do the same dive. That took courage. And he did the dive perfectly.

But the Russian diver was badly hurt. A week later he died. It was the first time such a terrible accident had ever happened at a diving meet. It reminded everyone how dangerous diving could be. Even very good divers could make very bad mistakes.

12.

Like hundreds of other athletes, Greg had been very disappointed when he didn't get to go to the Moscow Olympic Games. But the Olympics coming up in 1984 promised to make up for what he had missed. The '84 Olympics were being held in Los Angeles, California. The audience for all the events would be made up of Americans. All the U.S. athletes were looking forward to competing in front of their family and friends.

The opening ceremony of the games was thrilling. Tens of thousands filled the seats of the Los Angeles Coliseum. Hundreds of singers and musicians were on hand to entertain. Ath-

letes from all the countries taking part in the Olympics paraded around the track.

Finally it came time to light the Olympic flame. Before every Olympics a flaming torch is brought all the way from Greece, the home of the first Olympic Games. When the torch arrived at the stadium, the Games could officially begin. A lone runner appeared at the entrance to the stadium, holding the torch high. A granddaughter of Olympic hero Jesse Owens had been chosen to carry the torch on a lap around the track. It was a moving moment.

It had been eight years since Greg had competed in the Olympics. And the pressure was on. Diving had not always been one of the most popular Olympic sports. This year was different. Greg was expected to win a gold medal for the United States. There was even a chance he would win in springboard *and* platform diving. No one had done that since 1928. More than 13,000 fans crowded into the stands at the Olympic pool to see if Greg would succeed. Greg's former

Greg (second row, far right) and the rest of the U.S. Olympic diving team had high hopes for the Los Angeles games.

coach, Dr. Lee, had come to cheer him on. So had many of the divers he had beaten in the past.

The big crowds were exciting. But would they help Greg's chances or hurt them?

Diving takes a hundred percent concentration. If Greg's mind wandered, even for a second, he could easily get hurt.

So like most divers, Greg did his best to ignore the spectators. In between dives he left the pool area.

He didn't even want to know the score. That was for Coach O'Brien to worry about.

While his opponents dived, Greg sat in a quiet room. He would go over his next dive in his mind. Greg still picked songs to go with each of his dives. For the compulsory dives—the ones all the divers had to do—he chose classical music. For the harder dives, he chose popular songs. When he hummed the music, he would picture himself doing the dive perfectly.

The springboard event came first. Everything went smoothly. Greg did every one of his dives well. He finished more than ninety-two points ahead of the diver in second place. At last Greg had won a gold medal. At long last!

There was no time for Greg and Coach O'Brien to celebrate. The platform event was still ahead of them. Once again Greg started out well. He got through the first nine dives of the final round without making a serious mistake.

Greg soared to a gold medal in the springboard event.

Greg's tenth dive was one of his toughest. The music he thought of when he did it was his favorite song from the musical *The Wiz:* "Believe in Yourself."

As he climbed up the ladder, the song was running through Greg's mind. The 13,000 fans in the audience didn't make a sound.

Greg didn't know his exact score, but he knew he had been diving very well. He knew he had to be headed for a medal. Why was the crowd so quiet?

Greg was the only person in the pool area who didn't know that he was on his way to making diving history. He was far ahead of his nearest rival. He would win the gold medal even if he only got fives on his last dive. But he also had a chance to score the highest number of total points ever. To break the record, he needed a very good score on his final dive.

When Greg leaped from the platform, the crowd gasped.

His somersaults were perfect. The judges scored five 9.5s, one nine, and one perfect ten. The thousands who watched Greg's record-breaking performance would never forget it.

For Dr. Sammy Lee it was one of the most

thrilling moments in his life. "I don't think any diver will ever equal this," he said.

As Greg mounted the victory platform to receive his second gold, the crowd exploded with cheers. Greg had done it! Even the diver Greg

had beaten seemed excited. He called Greg Louganis "the best diver in the world."

After Los Angeles most people expected Greg to retire from diving. He had won more championships than any diver in history. Why keep training long hours day after day? Why keep dieting to stay in shape? Why risk getting hurt?

Greg thought about retiring. He bought a house on the beach, just where he had always wanted to live. He played a small part in a movie. He won a lead role in a professional dance performance. His jazz dancing and high leaps were the hit of the program.

Still, Greg just couldn't stay away from the pool. At first he dived just for fun. After a while he found himself thinking about ways to make his best dives even better. In his heart he knew that he really did not want to quit.

People started saying that Greg could win two more gold medals in the 1988 Olympics in Seoul, South Korea. Greg wasn't so sure. No one had ever come back to win both events again.

In 1988, Greg had his first leading role as a professional dancer.

He could only spend half as much time practicing, because he had to work on his dancing, too. If he took part in the Seoul Olympics, all the other divers would be out to beat him. Anything less than two gold medals would seem like a failure.

Greg decided to go ahead anyway. Winning wasn't his main reason for diving. Now he did it because he loved the sport.

Before Greg could go to Korea, he had to make the U.S. team. In one meet he entered, he came in second in each of three events. Greg tried to be a good loser. "Other divers have a right to win once in a while," he said. But in his heart he wondered if he had made a mistake by not retiring. By 1988 he would be twenty-eight years old. Maybe his best diving days were behind him. Greg went to Coach O'Brien for advice. "I'm still doubting myself," he confessed.

Ron O'Brien thought for a while. Then he said, "Well, if you don't have faith in yourself, have faith in me. I'll stand by you. We'll get through together."

After that Greg spent more time training. He did aerobic dancing and running to keep in condition. He even went to a sports-medicine clinic for testing. The doctors there found out that Greg could jump thirty inches into the air from a standing start. His muscles were like the muscles of a world-class sprinter.

But was all this enough to make history at the Seoul Olympics?

13.

The diving events at the Seoul Olympics opened with a touching ceremony. Dr. Sammy Lee, the coach who had helped Greg in 1976, had been invited to take part. Dressed up in a traditional Korean costume, Dr. Lee banged a big gong. Everyone cheered.

Dr. Lee was proud that the games were being held in his native land. He was especially happy because his most famous pupil would be diving again.

In Korea, Greg found himself competing against much younger divers. One Chinese diver, Xiong Ni, was just fourteen years old. That was half Greg's age. When Greg won his first

Olympic medal, Xiong Ni was only two years old!

Greg's first dives proved that he was still as graceful as ever. He made diving look like dancing. He was so graceful that some people called him "The Panther."

But the younger divers were thin. When they hit the water, they made hardly any splash. Now that Greg was older, he weighed more. It was harder for him to "punch a hole" in the water. Sometimes his wrists ached from the effort.

The contest started with the springboard. On the first day divers from each country did ten dives. Only the best would be in the finals.

Even though the springboard did not look as dangerous as the platform, most divers thought this event was more difficult. The bouncing board could be hard to control.

Greg started out well. Then it came time to do one of his trickiest dives. He had to make two and a half somersaults—in reverse. That wasn't easy to do off the springboard.

Greg jumped high into the air. But he did not jump out enough from the board. The mistake took just a split second.

Greg heard a loud noise. *Clank!* He realized the noise was the back of his head hitting the board.

Greg's head struck the edge of the board.

There was another smacking sound as Greg's body landed in the water.

The crowd gasped.

Greg got out of the pool without help. He knew everyone was watching. Even the TV cameras. He tried to smile. But inside he was shaking.

The judges put up their scores. Three of them gave Greg one point. One gave him half a point. Two other judges gave him a zero. Many of the fans groaned. Greg Louganis getting a zero!

Someone called a medic. He looked at Greg's head. It took four big stitches to close up the cut.

Many people who had seen the accident expected Greg to drop out of the contest. But minutes later there he was, back on the board again. The dive he had to do was even tougher than the one he had just missed. He patted his heart and smiled. Then he took off.

This time Greg's dive was almost perfect. The judges gave him high scores. The crowd went

After Greg hit his head, a meet official rushed to his side.

wild. They weren't just cheering the scores. They were cheering Greg for having the courage to come back at all.

Even with his accident Greg still made the finals.

14.

When he left the pool, Greg went straight to the hospital. A doctor stitched up his head again. Then he put a big patch over the cut.

That night Greg couldn't sleep. He had plenty of time to think about what went wrong. He figured that in nine years he had dived off the springboard about 180,000 times. In all that time he had never made such a bad mistake. True, he had hit the platform once. He had missed dives. But he had never hit the springboard.

What was the matter? Was he too old? Had his luck run out?

These thoughts made Greg feel afraid to dive

again. But he had been afraid before. And he had always overcome his fears.

"A little fear is okay," he decided. His mistake would just teach him to be more careful the next time. Controlling his fear gave him a goal.

The next morning Greg's jaw hurt. "I feel like I got punched out by Mike Tyson," he told a friend.

Many divers have good-luck charms. Greg's was his lucky teddy bear. The friend put a big patch on the back of the teddy bear's head—just like Greg's. When the other divers saw that bear, they knew Greg was not going to make things easy for them.

Greg did not even change his program. When it came time for his ninth dive, there was tension in the air. No one said anything out loud. But everyone knew this was the dive Greg had been trying to do when he hit the board. Was he going to have another accident?

Greg seemed to be the coolest person at the

pool. He hit the dive perfectly. Everyone cheered loudly. When the scores were added up, it was official. Greg had won the gold medal in springboard.

Even with stitches in his head, Greg still came back to win the gold.

A few days later it was time for the platform event. Here it was harder to keep up with some of the younger divers. Greg made the finals. But after nine out of ten dives he was still in second place. The fourteen-year-old Chinese diver was first. Greg was three points behind.

Greg's last dive was going to be the three and a half reverse tuck. This was still the hardest dive in the rule book . . . the one that had killed the Russian diver. Chances were it would also be the last dive of Greg Louganis's career.

To beat Xiong Ni, Greg would have to do the dive almost perfectly. Otherwise he would have to end his career in second place.

The tension was terrible. But Greg tried to keep calm. He remembered what he used to tell himself back when he first started going to diving meets—"My mother will still love me no matter what happens."

No one made a sound . . .

It was a long climb to the top of the platform. Xiong Ni of China was the diver just ahead of Greg.

Here is Greg right before he made his final dive.

Then he jumped. He jumped out just far enough to miss the tower. But not too far. It was his best dive of the day.

Greg looked at the scoreboard. He looked at his coach.

To win, he needed a total of **85.57** points.

The dive was good enough to put him one point ahead of Xiong Ni.

The judges wrote down their decisions. Then the computer figured out the total for the dive. It came to 86.70. Greg had beaten Xiong Ni by just one point.

When the total flashed on the board, Greg smiled. Then his eyes filled with tears. Coach O'Brien was crying too. He gave Greg a big hug.

Once again, Greg stood on the victory platform while "The Star-Spangled Banner" was played.

"You picked a hard way to do it," he said.

Greg and Coach O'Brien weren't the only ones with tears in their eyes. People in the audience were crying too. Even the Chinese coach said that Greg had taught everyone a lesson. He had shown the world that a champion never gives up.

15.

A few days later Greg stepped off the airplane that had brought him home from Korea.

He now held more titles than anyone in diving history. Besides his Olympic medals he had won forty-seven U.S. titles and 118 world-class diving events!

Many people said there would never be another diver as good. But Greg hoped that wasn't true. He wanted the sport of diving to keep getting better.

"I don't want to be remembered as the greatest diver who ever lived," he said. "I want to be able to *see* the greatest diver."

But Greg still had not won his last medal.

The U.S. athletes at the games were given a chance to vote for the athlete with the most spirit. The award went to Greg Louganis.

Greg came home from Seoul with two gold medals. He was looking forward to new challenges.